W9-CNR-354

FAMOUS MOVIE MONSTERS™

MEET THE MUMMY

The Rosen Publishing Group, Inc.
New York

SUSAN GORDON

To Parker

Published in 2005 by The Rosen Publishing Group, Inc.
29 East 21st Street, New York, NY 10010

First Edition

Library of Congress Cataloging-in-Publication Data

Gordon, Susan, 1968–
Meet the mummy/by Susan Gordon.
    p. cm.—(Famous movie monsters)
Includes bibliographical references and index.
ISBN 1-4042-0273-0 (lib. binding)
1. Mummy (Motion picture) I. Title. II. Series.
PN1997.M816G67 2005
791.43'72—dc22

2004020486

Manufactured in the United States of America

On the cover: Boris Karloff as the Mummy

J-NF

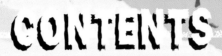

CONTENTS

CHAPTER 1

THE MUMMY

It is 1921, exactly one year before King Tutankhamen's tomb will be discovered. Archaeologists Dr. Muller, Sir Joseph Whemple, and young Ralph Norton are in an ancient burial tomb in Egypt. They have come from England to find Egyptian artifacts for the museum in Cairo, the capital of Egypt. They have just unearthed the 3,700-year-old tomb of Imhotep, a priest from an ancient Egyptian temple. Imhotep's grave still contains many Egyptian treasures, including a sarcophagus that holds his mummified body and a small golden casket. Inside the casket is the sacred Scroll of Troth, which has been locked away from prying hands and eyes for thousands of years.

Dr. Muller examines the mummy as Sir Joseph and Ralph look on. He soon realizes something is terribly wrong with the bandaged body.

"It looks like he died in some sensationally unpleasant manner," he tells the other two men. "The contorted muscles indicate that he struggled in the bandages."

Dr. Muller reads the chilling words on the mummy's sarcophagus aloud: "Death, eternal punishment, for anyone who opens this casket. In the name of Amon-Ra, king of the gods." He begins to realize that Imhotep is dangerously different from other mummies. He reads on and learns that the mummy they share a room with now was an ancient priest. Against the law of the Egyptian gods, the priest had dared to fall in love with the princess Ankhesenamen and tried to bring her back to life when she died. For that sacrilege the priest was buried alive, condemned to an eternity of suffering.

Dr. Muller and Sir Joseph soon decide to get away from the tomb's smothering air. They walk out among the rocks and sand of the Egyptian desert and talk. Sir Joseph says that the finds belong to the Cairo Museum now. The precious objects should be moved to the museum and studied in the name of science. Dr. Muller, however, knows that the ancient gods must be feared and respected. Sternly, he insists that these things should be left alone.

Meanwhile, inside the cavelike tomb, Ralph is filled with the thrill of discovery. He opens the box and removes the Scroll of Troth. By the flickering light of the gas lamp, he begins to decipher the ancient hieroglyphics.

Hypnotized by the millennia-old spell he has unleashed, he begins to read the ancient words. As he speaks, he does not notice the mummy's eyes slowly blinking behind him— alive with new life! He does not hear the rustling behind him as the mummy's linen wrappings scrape softly against the tomb floor for the first time in more than 3,000 years.

Suddenly, Imhotep's deathly cold hand is on the scroll beside him. Ralph whirls around in time to see the bandaged

Awakened after 3,000 years, the Mummy (Boris Karloff) emerges from his tomb, takes an ancient scroll from Ralph Norton (Bramwell Fletcher), and disappears into the night. Karloff appeared in more than 80 films before shooting to stardom with *Frankenstein* in 1931. His role in *The Mummy* followed just a year later.

body moving on its own through the tomb's door and into the night of modern Cairo.

Outside, Sir Joseph and Dr. Muller are startled by loud sounds coming from the tomb. Dr. Muller rushes back inside, and what he sees there horrifies him. The mummy and the scroll are gone! At the table, inches from the empty box that only minutes ago held the ancient Scroll of Troth, sits Ralph.

His eyes roll madly, his body shakes with hysterical laughter as he declares to his two colleagues, "He . . . he went for a little walk. You should have seen his face!"

*   *   *

More than ten years have now passed since that 1921 expedition was abandoned. Sir Joseph's son, Frank, is now the lead archaeologist of a team that has returned to Cairo. Frank's expedition isn't having much luck at all. He and Dr. Muller meet at headquarters to plan their next move.

Soon, there is a knock at the door. Outside stands a tall man—majestic, dignified, and strangely dressed in long white robes. The stranger introduces himself with a deep solemn voice: "I am Ardeth Bey." Beneath his old-fashioned cap, the stranger's face is lined with heavy, dusty wrinkles.

The mysterious Bey offers to help them unearth the most sensational find since King Tutankhamen. He will show them where to dig for the lost tomb of the princess Ankhesenamen.

Within a week, the princess is found at the exact spot Ardeth Bey promised she would be. The royal tomb is excavated and Ankhesenamen's mummified body and buried possessions are brought to the Cairo Museum.

*   *   *

It is the middle of summer in Cairo and Dr. Muller is hosting a cocktail party for the local and English personalities. The guest list includes the daughter of the English governor of Sudan, Helen Grosvenor. Helen's mother, a rich local woman from an ancient Egyptian family, died years before, leaving her half-Egyptian daughter to grow up among her father's British relatives and colleagues in Cairo.

Karloff stares menacingly as the Mummy. Because the actor had a darker skin tone than most Hollywood actors at the time, he was often cast in his early movies as Arabs or Native Americans.

At the party, Helen makes polite conversation with several people she knows. However, she moves restlessly, yearning to be somewhere else as she walks out onto one of the house's huge balconies, where the starry sky stretches from the sparkling lights of Cairo into the dark Egyptian desert. Soon, Dr. Muller joins her to marvel at the nighttime scene, but Helen confesses that she secretly despises her new city. "I hate this dreadful modern Cairo," she says. "How many people really see the true Egypt?"

Back inside, Frank has noticed Helen and asks Dr. Muller to introduce him to the beautiful yet mysterious dark-haired woman. But suddenly he notices her leaving. As if under a spell, Helen recovers her wrap from the party's coat check and glides to her car. She tells the driver, "To the museum!"

*   *   *

The museum, which has been closed for several hours, is empty of all visitors—except one. Ardeth Bey stands by Ankhesenamen's mummified body, reading from a scroll.

Meanwhile, Helen's car is racing toward the museum. Her car pulls up to the huge museum doors and she runs out, but the doors are tightly locked. Still hypnotized, she bangs on the door, but no one answers. Exhausted and disappointed, she collapses. Just then Frank, who has followed her from the party, arrives to catch her in his arms.

Inside the darkened museum, a guard has discovered Ardeth Bey holding the missing sacred scroll. He slowly moves toward the tall stranger. Suddenly, he freezes and grabs at his own neck. He cannot breathe! He falls to the floor, struggles in vain for air, and then is still.

The local police arrive to find the guard's dead body alone in the museum. The scroll is found nearby, and a policeman is dispatched to the Whemples' home to deliver the scroll to Sir Joseph for safekeeping.

Frank brings Helen to his home and he, Sir Joseph, and Dr. Muller gather around her in the drawing room. As the men discuss the night's events, Helen lies delirious on the Whemples' couch. She mutters bizarre words, and the men struggle to make sense of them. Suddenly, Sir Joseph understands. These words, he says, have not been heard on this earth for thousands of years. Helen is speaking an ancient Egyptian language!

Frank is left to watch over Helen while the two older men retire to Sir Joseph's study to talk. Helen soon wakes from the spell and finds herself alone with Frank. She seems angry, asking him about his archaeological projects. "How could you do that?" she asks him, appalled. "Don't you think opening ancient tombs is a sacrilege of the worst kind?"

At the Whemples' front door, the servant hears a light knock. He opens the door and falls to his knees in adoration of the man before him. Ardeth Bey walks past him and into the drawing room.

As Bey enters, Helen suddenly slips back into her trance. Enchanted, she rises to meet him. They stare into each other's eyes, oblivious to anyone else in the room.

"Have we met?" he asks her.

"I don't think I'd forget meeting you," she tells him. "I've never felt so alive."

Frank stands by helpless. Hearing a strange man's voice, Sir Joseph and Dr. Muller rush back from the study. Dr. Muller holds an old illustration of Imhotep, the ancient Egyptian priest who was buried alive thousands of years ago. Bey gazes at the picture, then instantly becomes furious. Dr. Muller's suspicions have been confirmed: Ardeth Bey is the resurrected Imhotep!

Filled with rage, Bey begins to recite an ancient spell to murder Sir Joseph. As the high priest recites the words, Dr. Muller threatens to destroy the Scroll of Troth. Bey suddenly stops his spell and turns, leaving the Whemple home.

Hidden away in his home in modern Cairo, Ardeth Bey leans over an enchanted pool. From the pool's waters, he conjures up Sir Joseph's face and mutters the words of an ancient ritual.

Miles away, alone in his study, Sir Joseph feels a sharp, tight pain in his chest that shoots through his left arm. He grits his teeth and curls up to ease some of the mind-numbing pain. But it's no use, he is suffering a fatal heart attack. Within seconds, he is dead.

Helen Grosvenor (Zita Johann) is entranced by the mysterious Ardeth Bey (Boris Karloff). A long reincarnation scene that was very important to the plot was not allowed into the final movie because scenes involving reincarnation were banned by censors. This angered Johann, who strongly believed in reincarnation.

Moments later, Sir Joseph's servant slips past the dead body and gathers the sacred Scroll of Troth. He will bring it to his new master's home, as he's been commanded to do.

Several days have passed since Sir Joseph was found dead. At her home, Helen is waiting for Frank. She decides to take a walk. Outside, she is mysteriously and helplessly drawn to a house in Cairo. Bey is waiting for her there. He leads her

to his magical pool and casts another spell. The waters stir and after a moment reveal terrifying scenes of the princess Ankhesenamen's death and Imhotep's punishment.

Finally, Helen understands. She is the reincarnation of Imhotep's long-lost love, the princess Ankhesenamen! Disguised as Ardeth Bey, Imhotep has returned from the dead to kill and mummify her. He will then bring her back to life with the Scroll of Troth so she can live forever as Ankhesenamen.

Helen pleads with him. "I'm young!" she begs. "I loved you once, but now you belong with the dead. I am Ankhesenamen, but I . . . I'm somebody else, too. I want to live!"

But Bey has been dreaming of this moment for more than 3,000 years. "For thy sake I was buried alive," he tells Helen. "Let the deed be done." He raises an ancient jeweled dagger and moves toward her.

In terror, Helen prays to a statue of Isis, an ancient Egyptian goddess, which stands near the mummy's pool. Suddenly, the door breaks open and Frank rushes in. Bey raises his hand in a powerful gesture that stops Frank before he reaches Helen.

Bey holds the dagger above Helen's heart. She is screaming now, begging Isis to save her from this horrible fate. Suddenly she faints, overcome with fear.

Just then, the statue of Isis comes to life and raises its hand, pointing directly at Bey. The ancient priest moans in

Ardeth Bey stares intently into the enchanted pool in which he casts spells. *The Mummy* was the first directing assignment for acclaimed cinematographer Karl Freund, who employed the same elegant horror style in *The Mummy* that he used when shooting *Dracula* (1931).

Helen pleads with Ardeth Bey to spare her life. In many ways, the storyline of *The Mummy* is similar to that of *Dracula*. Both films feature immortal men who are in love with women living in the modern world. The idea of a monster who can feel emotion was very popular with movie audiences at the time.

fear of Isis's wrath. He falls to the ground, his body convulsing, and then it is all over. For a moment there is a small pile of dust on the floor where Imhotep once stood. And then the dust is gone, too, disintegrated as the Scroll of Troth burns.

Frank rushes to Helen's side, taking her in his arms. He gently calls her back to life, back to the modern world.

CHAPTER 2

THE MAKING OF THE MUMMY

In 1932, when *The Mummy* opened in theaters across the United States, the country was in the throes of the Great Depression (1929–1939). At the time, Universal Studios, which produced *The Mummy*, was unquestionably the leading American producer of horror films. *Dracula*, the first wildly successful American horror film, and its rapid and equally successful follow-up, *Frankenstein*, had been released by Universal in 1931, one year before the unveiling of *The Mummy*.

Audiences had been given their first taste of the tall, brooding Boris Karloff when he played the monster in Universal's *Frankenstein*. His intense, mesmerizing on-screen presence had kept audiences' eyes glued to the movie screen. In *Frankenstein*, Karloff was billed without a name at all, simply as "?." By the time *The Mummy* audiences were shaking in their movie theater seats, however, Karloff had already begun his rapid climb to horror stardom. For his role in *The Mummy*, he was publicized as "Karloff the Uncanny," becoming the first Hollywood actor to be billed by his last name alone. To many critics, the Imhotep/Ardeth Bey role remains the best work of Karloff's acting career. As in *Frankenstein*, his towering figure and silent, brooding air made him a natural to play the terrifying yet tragic mummy.

HOLLYWOOD MONSTER MONEY

The stock market crash of 1929 that began the United States' Great Depression had a profound effect on the U.S. movie industry. Horror films offered audiences a chance to escape their daily economic hard-ships and to redirect their daily worries elsewhere for an hour or so. These films proved to be an enor-mously successful genre for the movie industry. Box-office ticket sales from *Dracula* and *Frankenstein* added up to enough money to save Universal Studios from financial ruin. This finan-cial success sparked a movie monster craze that continues to ebb and flow to this day.

Though Boris Karloff had been an unknown actor just a few years earlier, he had become such a big star after *Frankenstein* that posters for *The Mummy* referred to him simply as Karloff the Uncanny.

Eager to replay its success with *Dracula* and *Frankenstein*, Universal began looking to produce another movie that would guarantee audiences as well as their precious few entertainment dollars.

HOW TO WRITE A MUMMY

The mixture of a love story and horror that was so effective in *Dracula* seemed to be the formula for success for which Universal had been searching. In 1931, when work on the mummy movie began, the studio originally reworked the *Dracula* tale simply by changing the setting from Transylvania and London to Egypt.

Throughout the late 1920s and beyond, America was hypnotized by Egyptology, the study of ancient Egyptian artifacts. During that decade, several major archaeological discoveries were made that uncovered mysterious burial sites. Newspapers carried tales of strange Egyptian rituals and curses back to the American public. At the same time, Universal wanted the *Dracula* follow-up to be another successful tale of love and horror. The studio's decision to capitalize on the popular fascination with Egypt was to be a quick icing on the cake.

Writing the script for the mummy story turned out to be a much longer process than originally planned. In the end, the script was rewritten twice. The original story for the film was penned by magazine writer Nina Wilcox Putnam and was based on the real-life, eighteenth-century Italian alchemist Alessandro di Conte Cagliostro, who was said to have traveled around the world, studying the occult.

Once Universal Studios approved Putnam's story, the job of making it ready for the screen fell to John Balderston. Balderston had previously written the Broadway version of the *Dracula* and *Frankenstein* film scripts. He was also a reporter who covered the discovery of King Tut's tomb in 1922, a discovery that captivated imaginations around the world and helped spark the Egyptology craze. Balderston used some small pieces of the original Putnam story to develop the screenplay that Universal ultimately used for *The Mummy*.

As the script was being rewritten, it went through various name changes. Originally titled *Cagliostro* by Putnam, it was then called *King of the Dead*. Balderston named his mummy Imhotep, after the real-life ancient Egyptian architect who designed the first pyramid. The film's title was then changed to *Im-Ho-Tep* and, finally, to *The Mummy*.

TELL A GOOD STORY TWICE

Balderston's screenplay so closely followed the *Dracula* script that, except for *The Mummy's* flashbacks to ancient Egypt, *Dracula* and *The Mummy* are almost the same film. Many of the set props used in *Dracula* were also used in *The Mummy*. Additionally, several of *Dracula's* actors reappear in similar roles in this film. David Manners, *Dracula's* Jonathan Harker, plays Frank, Helen's modern-day boyfriend and the monster's rival for her affections in *The Mummy*. Edward Van Sloan's Dr. Muller is essentially a replay of Van Sloan's vampire-hunting Dr. Van Helsing character in *Dracula*.

Karl Freund, the cinematographer of *Dracula*, was offered his first directorial job with *The Mummy*. Riding high off his success with *Dracula*, he jumped at his first chance to direct a film. And not just any film, but a monster movie that might become the next enormously successful Hollywood event.

FINDING THE MUMMY

Balderston's script had been written for Bela Lugosi, *Dracula's* star, to play the role of Imhotep. But Lugosi eventually turned down the role, worried that the heavy makeup required to play the ancient monster would make him unrecognizable to his fans. *The Mummy* was finally filmed with Boris Karloff in the leading role instead.

Karloff's mummy is for all intents and purposes a modern monster. The tales of *Dracula* and *Frankenstein* are based on centuries-old literary works. The story of *The Wolf Man*, another popular Universal monster, is based on centuries of local legends and folklore. Until the Egyptology craze in America and England began in the late nineteenth century, Egyptian mummies, removed as they were from Western traditions, had never been scary figures. More than anything else, it was the media's sensational response to the 1922 discovery of King Tutankhamen's tomb that brought mummies to life in the Western imagination.

MONSTROUS MAKEUP

In the film, it takes less than three minutes for the mummy to come to life. But it took Universal Studio's star makeup

BORIS KARLOFF

Karloff the Uncanny was born William Henry Pratt, in London, on November 23, 1887. He attended London University, with the intent of becoming a diplomat but instead became an actor. In 1908, he moved to the United States and changed his name to Boris Karloff, which he considered a more suitable name for an actor. He appeared in almost eighty films before landing the lead in *Frankenstein*. By the time he became famous, he was forty-four years old, a late bloomer by Hollywood standards. Because he had a darker skin tone than many other Hollywood actors (his mother was part East Indian), Karloff was often cast as an Arab or Native American in silent films.

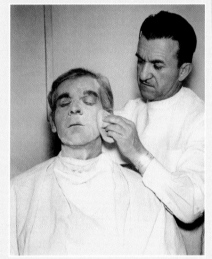

Makeup artist Jack Pierce works on Boris Karloff. The actor had to wear his heavy mummy makeup for eight hours to film the movie's short opening sequence.

Although Karloff is usually pictured as a very large man, he was actually of slim build and stood only five feet, ten inches (1.8 meters) tall. He had to wear bulky lifts and padding and be shot from certain camera angles in order to convincingly play Universal's towering monsters. And unlike the scary image he presented in most of his films, Karloff was a quiet, bookish man who was particularly fond of children. In 1966, he supplied the voice for both the Grinch and the narrator for the animated version of Dr. Seuss's *How the Grinch Stole Christmas*. This work would earn him the 1968 Grammy Award for Best Album for Children.

artist Jack Pierce many hours to create the ancient monster. Pierce used a painstaking process that employed layers of makeup and thin cotton strips and more than 150 yards (137 m) of linen that covered every inch of Karloff's body (including his eyelids).

Karloff wore the dusty makeup for eight hours in order to film the short opening scene of the movie. The makeup for Ardeth Bey, the revived mummy who searched the streets of modern Egypt for his ancient love, took less time to create but was no less genius in its application. In today's horror films, monsters are created from foam rubber in a separate makeup studio for many days and then fitted to

Lon Chaney Jr. holds his nose as Jack Pierce applies the foul-smelling makeup used to transform the actor into Kharis in *The Mummy's Ghost* (1944). The film was one of several sequels to *The Mummy* that Universal released following the success of the original.

the actor at the last minute. But in the 1930s, makeup for special effects was applied in many layers directly to the actor's face over long periods of time.

Pierce had previously transformed Karloff into Frankenstein's monster and created many other famous monsters for the screen, including the Wolf Man and the Invisible

Man. Pierce had also been called upon to work on *Dracula*. But the film's star, Bela Lugosi, was a theater actor who always did his own makeup, and he refused to let Pierce work on him. For *Dracula*, the famous makeup artist had to settle for designing the look of Lugosi's Count Dracula and many of the female characters in the vampire movie. Although *Dracula* and *Frankenstein* became more popular films than *The Mummy*, Pierce considered *The Mummy* his best work.

WAKING THE MUMMY

Three major themes in *The Mummy* are reincarnation, undying love, and, most importantly, sleepwalking, the same themes that had made Universal's *Dracula* a huge success one year earlier. *Dracula* was *The Mummy*'s precursor not only in storyline and actors, but also in themes and imagery.

The first film version of the story of Dracula was *Nosferatu*, which was made in Germany in 1922. *Nosferatu*'s success was due largely to its use of dark, haunting imagery. The image of the vampire slowly stalking its prey through the night occurs throughout the film, bringing to mind the slow, silent movements of a sleepwalker. At the time, in Germany, sleepwalking was a metaphor for military conscription, in which civilian men were dragged off the streets and forced to fight for Germany in World War I (1914–1918).

Years later, during the Great Depression, Americans were confronted daily with visions of men standing all day in soup lines that ran blocks long. *The Mummy*'s sleepwalking images

Long bread lines like these were familiar sights for most Americans during the Great Depression. The sleepwalking images featured in *The Mummy* mirrored these long, winding lines of barely moving unemployed men and women.

easily fit 1932 America's nightmare images of those barely moving lines of shuffling and unemployed men and women.

Universal's *Dracula* was released during the first years of the Great Depression and represented those first dark days of the U.S. stock market crash. *The Mummy* carried its forerunner's themes right into the heart of the worst days of America's decadelong Depression era.

CHAPTER 3

THE MUMMY *AND THE MYTH*

In 1799, the Rosetta stone was found in Egypt. This stone, which was carved with writing in both Egyptian and Greek, allowed scholars to decipher Egyptian hieroglyphics and to translate early Egyptian history and culture to a general audience. With the subsequent discoveries of ancient texts and tombs (especially the 1922 discovery of King Tutankhamen's tomb), Egyptology became a popular obsession in the United States and England. As they do today, people began to buy and collect miniature replicas of Egyptian artifacts and art with Egyptian themes. The Egyptology craze, however, had little to do with discovering true Egyptian culture.

In the early twentieth century, people living in the United States and England were reeling from massive cultural and economic change brought on by industrialization. Egyptology became a way for Western audiences to deal with their own rapidly changing societies. As modern empires, the United States and England could look to the 5,000-year-old Egypt as a model of a solid, enduring society.

EGYPT AND THE WEST

Egypt, located in North Africa, has been a nation for more than 5,000 years. Until about 2,000 years ago, it was a vast empire with a rich culture, literature, and political system that influenced and shaped much of the known world at the time. For centuries after its fall as an empire, Egypt continued to be a cultural force. Many things we use today originated in this part of the world, with eyeglasses and libraries being just two of the things handed down to us from Egypt.

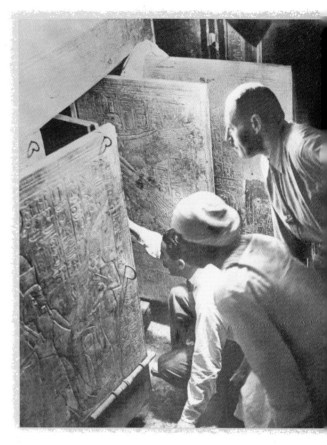

Howard Carter *(kneeling)* and his fellow archaeologists discover the tomb of Tutankhamen in Thebes, Egypt, in 1922. This discovery helped fuel the Egyptology craze that was sweeping through the United States and England since the 1800s.

By the nineteenth century, however, to the Western world, Egypt came to stand as something other than simply another country in North Africa. At that time, the United States and England were leaders of the Western world. The rapidly developing technology of their newly industrialized world was seen as powerful, mysterious, and sometimes dangerous. The Egyptology craze cast Egypt as dark, mysterious, and dangerous as well. And at the same time, cinema, a brand-new form of technology and entertainment, was rapidly becoming the newest popular craze.

EGYPT AND THE CINEMA

In the late 1800s, as the obsession with all things Egyptian was becoming more commonplace, the cinema was born. Now, movies allowed people to "watch" stories. Some of these stories offered explanations, reassurance, and warnings about the new industrial world. Cinema also offered people an escape from modern anxieties. Film was the perfect medium with which to explore the American and English obsession with light cast into dark Egyptian tombs. Early movies, such as England's *Wanted—A Mummy* (1910), and two American films both titled *The Mummy* and both released in 1911, cast Egypt as a mysterious culture of death, ghostlike, and dark. Movie audiences were invited to join explorers as they ventured into these forgotten and forbidden tombs.

The advent of film and the Western fascination with ancient Egypt worked perfectly together. Both film and Egypt were commonly seen as mysterious, silent worlds that spoke through images, warning audiences of the dire consequences of irresponsible scientific inquiry. Audiences could think of the chemicals used for mummification and those for developing film as similar technologies. And the film projector, which projected images of another world, could be imagined as the hole broken in a tomb's wall upon first discovery. People could now come to darkened movie theaters to watch the new and fun technology of film.

TALKING AT THE MOVIES

Early films often used Egypt as subject matter and as location, further linking the West's fascination with Egyptology and the birth and development of cinema. By 1915, at least four film companies had sent crews to Egypt. Between 1909 and 1915, almost a dozen mummy movies, including *The Egyptian Mummy* (1914) were made in the United States. Films at this point were still silent films. They relied on images and written cues to stimulate the audience's imagination.

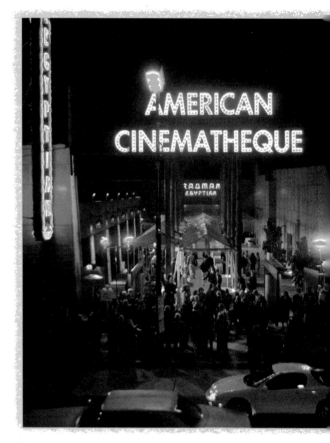

The influence of the Egyptology craze can be seen in Grauman's Egyptian Theatre, which opened in Hollywood in 1922, the same year that Tutankhamen's tomb was discovered.

But on October 6, 1927, the silent film era ended. That night, *The Jazz Singer*, featuring the first voice in a film, premiered in New York City and introduced "talkies" to the world. From that moment on, films would be matched with sound so that audiences could hear the characters on the screen speak. Also music and sound effects could be added to heighten drama. The draw of the cinema, already so enticing, was now practically irresistible. Box-office receipts flooded in, and film became a more and more popular art form.

As film became more widespread and affordable, the relationship between cinema as a Western art form and the West's obsession with Egyptology would come to a close as well. Along with several other countries, modern Egypt began to distribute its own films. Egypt, which was once silent and mysterious to U.S. and British moviegoers, finally gave those audiences a voice and language of its own to contend with. With the release of now-classic Egyptian films such as director Kamal Salim's *Determination* (1939), the mysterious shroud with which the West had once covered Egypt was finally lifted.

THE KING'S CURSE

In 1922, ten years before the release of Universal's *The Mummy*, British archaeologists searching for ancient treasures in Egypt on behalf of the British Museum made an earth-shaking discovery in the Valley of the Kings. Led by Howard Carter, an English Egyptologist, and his benefactor, Lord Carnarvon, the

Pictured here is the funeral mask of King Tutankhamen, created circa 1320 BC. The discovery of Tutankhamen's tomb inspired the idea of the Mummy's curse.

British team uncovered the tomb of King Tutankhamen, an ancient Egyptian king who had died more than 3,000 years ago.

The finding of King Tut's tomb fascinated the entire world and produced legends worthy of both ancient Egypt and modern cinema. An ancient curse was invented and swiftly carried into popular imaginations by the front pages of several newspapers. That curse jumped into the worldwide spotlight when Lord Carnarvon died just seven weeks after he and Carter discovered King Tut's tomb. All together, at least fourteen people involved with the digging expedition died within the year from presumably mysterious causes (five of the fourteen were actually present the moment King Tut's

HOW TO MAKE A MUMMY

To mummify a dead body, the ancient Egyptians removed every organ except the heart. Even the brain was removed, by slowly pulling it out through one nostril. The hollowed-out body was rubbed inside and out with salt (to dry it out) and left alone for more than a month. Then the dried-out body was treated with spices, salts, wine, and resin. Finally, it was stuffed with linen and sand and wrapped in linen bandages. The organs were preserved in jars, so that the deceased could use them again in the afterworld (for the same reason, the mummy's jewelry, clothes, food, and furniture were also left in his or her tomb).

According to Egyptian legend, the mummy would be sent on to the afterworld with its heart still inside the body. The ancient Egyptians believed that a mummy's heart would be weighed by the gods. A heart as light as a feather meant that the person had lived virtuously and, therefore, could be granted eternal life.

tomb was discovered). Although several of these people were quite elderly or ill at the time, the "mysterious" deaths led many people to believe in a curse that would kill anyone who disturbed the king in his sacred tomb. Newspapers and books of the time quickly followed up on this story, circulating many versions of it to an American and British public already fascinated by the supposedly exotic lands of Egypt.

STEALING EGYPT

While the goal of archaeologists is to remove ancient artifacts in the name of science, tomb raiders take those artifacts illegally and sell them. In a tomb raider's hands, many price-less treasures are often damaged and rarely end up in museums, where the public can enjoy and learn about these long-lost cultures. While it is true that many Egyptian tomb raiders faced terrible punishment during ancient times, this retaliation had little to do with any supernatural cause. If caught, most robbers were executed not for sacrilege or for disturbing the dead, but for stealing.

In its own way, the media would also carry off with what it could of the ancient Egyptian finds. Tales of ancient Egyptian curses, many exaggerated or outright made up, were easily found in contemporary American and British newspapers and books, and in the newly born cinema industry. By the time Universal realized *Dracula*'s unheard-of success in 1931, the myth of the mummy's curse was already well established in popular imaginations. It seemed only natural for a film studio to capitalize on real-life newspaper

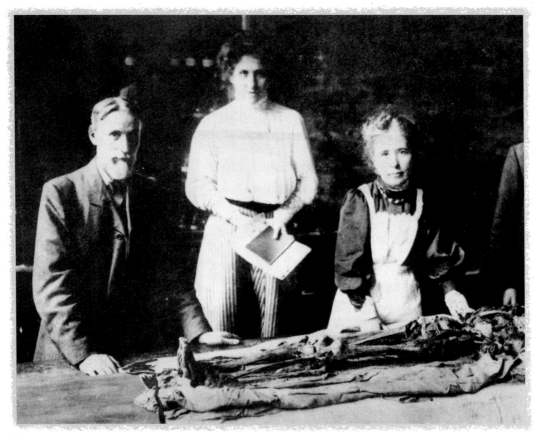

This 1898 monochrome photo shows scientists at Manchester University unwrapping a mummy. The group is led by Dr. Margaret A. Murray *(right)*, who was one of the first Egyptologists.

headlines, and reports on the mummy's curse were still among the most thrilling and sensational of the time.

THE MUMMY'S CURSE

The story of the mummy's curse actually began even earlier than the discovery of King Tut's tomb in 1922. It began as a story about revenge with the first version of the tale appearing almost 100 years before Lord Carnarvon's discovery.

In 1821, a stage show took place near London's Piccadilly Circus. As part of the show, Egyptian mummies were unwrapped in front of an audience already fascinated by the supposed mysteries of ancient Egypt. Inspired by the show, twenty-five-year-old British writer Jane Loudon wrote *The Mummy!: A Tale of the Twenty-second Century.* This story is now considered the first science-fiction story written by a woman. In Loudon's tale, a mummy comes back to life in the twenty-second century to seek revenge on a young scholarly man who is very much like Frank Whemple.

By the mid-nineteenth century, the character of the vengeful mummy had given way to the legend of the mummy's curse. In the imaginations of people in the West, ancient Egypt was a mysterious and dangerous place. Many people thought that modern Egypt still held some of that danger for Westerners who visited it. American audiences were hungry for any entertainment that could satisfy this popular curiosity with a country most of them could never hope to visit.

In 1869, American author Louisa May Alcott, who also wrote the immensely popular *Little Women*, wrote a short story called *Lost in a Pyramid or, the Mummy's Curse.* In Alcott's story, a man sets a mummified priestess on fire so that he can explore the darkened rooms inside a pyramid. When he presents the stolen treasures to his fiancée back home in England, the mummy's promise of revenge, or curse, comes true and his bride-to-be immediately turns into a mummy. In Alcott's story, the idea of the mummy's revenge becomes the tale of the mummy's curse.

The curse motif was expanded upon by other British and U.S. novelists for the next fifty years. The most noteworthy of these stories is Sir Arthur Conan Doyle's *Lot No. 249* (1892).

By the time Carter and Carnarvon entered Tutankhamen's real-life burial chamber in 1922, the idea of a mummy's curse was a popular horror device. And when successful British fantasy and science-fiction writer Marie Corelli dramatically warned in 1923 that "the most dire punishment follows any rash intruder into a sealed tomb," newspapers quickly quoted her. In the minds of literary and film audiences, her imaginative warning soon became a real inscription telling of an ancient curse that would strike down anyone who dared disturb King Tutankhamen's burial chamber.

UNIVERSAL'S MONSTERS

Perhaps the greatest influential force in creating Universal Studio's *The Mummy* was the ongoing financial and cultural success the Hollywood studio found with its previous movie monsters. In 1931, *Dracula* was a sudden, unexpected financial success. *Frankenstein* followed quickly that same year and was yet another astounding artistic, cinematic, and above all, financial accomplishment. Together, these two films launched Bela Lugosi's and Boris Karloff's careers as well as Universal's formula for cinematic success.

CHAPTER 4

THE MUMMY'S LEGACY

The first "monster movies" were short silent films made at the end of the nineteenth century. Then the groundbreaking *Nosferatu*, a silent feature-length film, was produced in Germany in 1922. *Nosferatu* was a chilling vampire tale that borrowed heavily from Bram Stoker's novel *Dracula*. The movie was innovative because it used images in a new, powerful way. *Nosferatu* terrified audiences, not with blood and gore but with subtle emotional and psychological devices.

Universal Studios completed its first movie in 1923. That film was *The Hunchback of Notre Dame*, a horror flick based on the 1831 book of the same name by French author Victor Hugo. The star of this movie became the first American horror film star, Lon Chaney. He was also known as the "Man of a Thousand Faces" and played twisted characters in many films, including *The Phantom of the Opera* and *London After Midnight*. With *The Hunchback of Notre Dame*, Universal staked its claim as master of what would become an indispensable movie genre: the horror film. Once set in that direction, Universal would go on to produce some of the most influential horror films of all time.

The painstaking attention and amount of time that makeup artist Jack Pierce devoted to transforming Karloff into both the frightening Imhotep and the underspoken, yet menacing Ardeth Bey, set a new standard in filmmaking. In terms of its technological and artistic achievements, *The Mummy* was a true genre-setter and had a profound influence on audiences' expectations for future Hollywood films.

TELLING *THE MUMMY* AGAIN AND AGAIN

The posters of Universal's original *The Mummy* led audiences to believe Karloff was playing a terrifying, bandaged mummy madly attacking people, while remaining frighteningly indestructible and unstoppable. In the film, however, the power of Universal's first mummy is much more subtle: he spends the greater part of the film reincarnated as the high priest he once was, executing his enemies and bending others to his will through hypnosis. But throughout the years, sequels and spin-off films would pick up on the action-filled promises made by the original film's title and posters.

In the 1940s, there were numerous sequels and remakes of horror films, perhaps more than in any other decade so far. An important mummy sequel was Universal's 1940 film *The Mummy's Hand*, in which a new mummy character named Kharis was introduced to American audiences. In 1942's *The Mummy's Tomb*, Kharis returned, this time played by Lon Chaney Jr., the son of the famous actor, who

The Mummy's Hand (1940) starred *(from left)* George Zucco, Peggy Moran, and Tom Tyler as the Mummy. In subsequent films, famed horror star Lon Chaney Jr. would take over the role of the Mummy.

was already well-known for his leading role in Universal's 1941 *The Wolf Man*. Chaney Jr. would go on to star in *The Mummy's Ghost* and *The Mummy's Curse*, both released by Universal Studios in 1944. As the monster craze waned in the late 1940s, science fiction films replaced the monsters, who had become more funny than scary to audiences.

The more famous movie monsters then moved into new film genres, such as comedy. In 1949, a direct spoof on

HAMMER FILMS REVIVES THE MUMMY

In the 1950s, the British production company Hammer Films revived the monster movie genre. Horror films had been losing both popularity and money-making power to the new genre of science fiction. Hammer brought Universal's most popular monsters, including Dracula and the Mummy, back to life. This time, however, the old monsters moved in sharp and vibrant color on the big screen. In Hammer's hands, monster movies became bloody, over-the-top affairs, while also preserving the subtle psychological horror tactics that Universal had used so well in the original

films. Peter Cushing and Christopher Lee were Hammer's most famous rivaling duo. In many ways, they echoed the tensions between Universal's greatest stars, Boris Karloff and Bela Lugosi.

In 1959, Hammer Films released *The Mummy*, directed by Terence Fisher. In this reworking of Universal's classic film, Christopher Lee plays the towering mummy Kharis. Kharis's object of

Christopher Lee battles Peter Cushing in *The Mummy* (1959), a film many consider to be the best movie Hammer Films ever made.

revenge, the archaeologist John Banning, is played by Peter Cushing. Many consider this film to be both the best mummy film and the best movie Hammer Films ever made. As with Hammer's other monster remakes, the 1959 *Mummy* held true to the subtle touch of the original, while successfully transforming the Mummy into an inarticulate, murderous monster. The Hammer film is perhaps best remembered for its terrifying off-camera scene in which the high priest Kharis's tongue is slashed out.

Though the first mummy remake was panned by the critics, the film made a lot of money, prompting Universal to plan a sequel. Like its predecessor, *The Mummy Returns*, shown above, was a commercial success but a critical flop. Stephen Sommers, the director of both films, also used old movie monsters for his 2004 hit, *Van Helsing*. That film featured Dracula, Frankenstein's monster, and the Wolf Man.

Universal's mummy spawned the popular comedy duo Bud Abbott and Lou Costello's *Abbott and Costello Meet the Killer, Boris Karloff*. A few years later the duo starred again in *Abbott and Costello Meet the Mummy* (1955). Abbott and Costello cornered the new horror spoof market and were pitted against Universal's most famous monsters in many films.

THE MODERN MUMMY

In 1999, director Stephen Sommers teamed up with Universal Studios for another remake of the original 1932 film. Sommers's *The Mummy* featured Brendan Fraser as the archaeologist who discovers Imhotep's tomb. This new film tried to combine the best of both worlds, with impressive digital effects and the return of the modern-day Ardeth Bey character. While the movie was a major financial success, enticing audiences with impressive sets and breathtaking special effects, it was a critical flop. But, as often happens in Hollywood, box-office receipts are more important than critical reviews, and two years later Brendan Fraser reappeared in Sommers's sequel *The Mummy Returns*.

Universal's careful subtlety, which worked so well to terrify audiences in 1932, was completely lacking in these two films. Flashy digital effects replaced haunting shadows; mysterious, invisible agents of the mummy's curse were replaced by bloody battle scenes between huge armies. In the end, Sommers's follow-up film suffered the same critical fate as his 1999 remake.

When *The Mummy* was released in 1932, it became clear that from then on the world would see Universal as an authority on the finest developments in the horror film genre. While Karloff's terrifying and refined monster has often faded into the background during the more than seventy years since its first release, it has also returned again and again to redefine the horror film genre from which it came.

FILMOGRAPHY

Mummy of the King Ramsees (1909). One of the first silent mummy films. Between 1909 and 1915, several silent films appeared in theaters. Many are titled simply *The Mummy* and *The Egyptian Mummy*.

The Mummy (1932). Universal Studios's mummy hit stars Boris Karloff who is billed as "Karloff the Uncanny."

The Mummy's Tomb (1942). Universal Studios releases the second of its Kharis the mummy films, this one starring Lon Chaney Jr. The first Kharis film went relatively unnoticed by both critics and the public.

The Mummy's Ghost and *The Mummy's Curse* (1944). Lon Chaney Jr. stars in two more of Universal's Kharis sequels.

Abbott and Costello Meet the Mummy (1955). Universal spoofs its own monster.

The Aztec Mummy, *The Robot Vs. the Aztec Mummy*, and *The Curse of the Aztec Mummy* (1957–1959). Three Mexican mummy films are released.

The Mummy (1959). British Hammer Films takes on the Universal classic film starring the famous Christopher Lee/Peter Cushing horror team. This is the first of several mummy-themed Hammer films. Many critics consider this the best mummy and best Hammer movie made yet.

The Curse of the Mummy's Tomb (1964). Hammer Films continues its mummy formula, without the Cushing/Lee team.

Bram Stoker's The Mummy (1997). A loose adaptation of Stoker's *The Jewel of the Seven Stars* stars Louis Gossett Jr. as the man who discovers the mummy's tomb.

The Mummy (1999). Universal Studios hires Stephen Sommers to direct *The Mummy*, a grandiose but poorly received remake of the 1932 original. The film stars Brendan Fraser.

The Mummy Returns (2001). Sommers follows up his 1999 film with Brendan Fraser again in the starring role. This film is a critical flop as well.

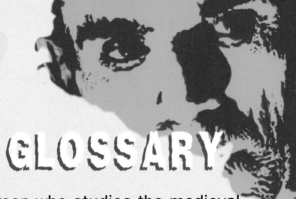

GLOSSARY

alchemist A person who studies the medieval science of alchemy. Alchemists sought to turn cheap metals into precious gold and to find a way to live forever.

cinematographer A movie cameraman or camerawoman who is largely responsible for the way a movie looks onscreen.

contemporary Existing or occurring at the same time.

empire A large number of people under one ruler; also a territory of land under the control of a monarch.

excavate To dig up something that was buried.

folklore Traditional tales, sayings, and art forms preserved among a culture.

genre A category of art (such as film, literature, or music) that has a particular style, form, or content.

hieroglyphics A form of writing that uses more than 700 pictures for different words and sounds.

hypnosis A trancelike state that resembles sleep. Someone under hypnosis readily obeys the hypnotizer's suggestions or commands and often appears to be sleepwalking.

industrialization A time of rapid expansion through the introduction of major inventions and industry.

Isis An Egyptian nature goddess; the wife of Osiris.

metaphor A figure of speech in which a word meaning one thing is used to mean another idea. A metaphor is used to suggest similarities between two different words or ideas.

motif A dominant, recurring, or central theme.

occult Relating to or dealing with supernatural powers or the secret knowledge of them.

parody To make fun of someone or something by imitating.

reincarnation Being born again in a new body.

sacrilege Gross disrespect of a sacred person, place, or thing.

sarcophagus A small building of carved stone made to be a grave.

spoof A light, humorous parody.

tomb raider Someone who steal objects from graves.

Victorian Having to do with the time when Queen Victoria ruled England (1837–1901), or with the standards or ideals of that time.

FOR MORE INFORMATION

American Film Institute
2021 N. Western Avenue
Los Angeles, CA 90027
(323) 856-7600
Web site: http://www.afi.com

American Research Center in Egypt
Emory University Briarcliff Campus
1256 Briarcliff Road NE
Building A, Suite 423W
Atlanta, GA 30306
(404) 712-9854
Web site: http://www.arce.org

WEB SITES

Due to the changing nature of Internet links, the Rosen
Publishing Group, Inc., has developed an online list of Web
sites related to the subject of this book. This site is updated
regularly. Please use this link to access the list:

http://www.rosenlinks.com/famm/memu

FOR FURTHER READING AND VIEWING

BOOKS

El Mahdy, Christine. *Mummies, Myth and Magic in Ancient Egypt*, reprint edition. London: Thames & Hudson, 1991.

Feramisco, Thomas, and Peggy Moran Koster. *The Mummy Unwrapped: Scenes Left on Universal's Cutting Room Floor*. Jefferson, NC: McFarland & Company, 2003.

Rice, Anne. *The Mummy*, reprint edition. New York: Ballantine Books, 1991.

Skal, David J. *The Monster Show: A Cultural History of Horror*. London: Faber & Faber, 2001.

FILMS

The Mummy, directed by Karl Freund. Universal Studios, 1932. DVD.

The Mummy's Tomb, directed by Harold Young. Universal Studios, 1942. VHS.

Abbott and Costello Meet the Killer, Boris Karloff, directed by Charles Barton. Universal Studios, 1949. VHS.

The Mummy, directed by Terence Fisher. Hammer Films, 1959. DVD.

The Mummy, directed by Stephen Sommers. Universal Studios, 1999. DVD.

BIBLIOGRAPHY

Bernstein, Matthew, and Gaylyn Studlar, eds.
Visions of the East: Orientalism in Film.
Piscataway, NJ: Rutgers University Press, 1997.

Shaheen, Jack. *Reel Bad Arabs: How Hollywood Vilifies a People.* Northampton, MA: Interlink Publishing Group, 2001.

Skal, David J. *The Monster Show: A Cultural History of Horror.* London: Faber & Faber, 2001.

Skal, David J. "Mummy Dearest: A Horror Tradition Unearthed." Hollywood, CA: Universal Studios, 2001. VHS.

INDEX

ABOUT THE AUTHOR

Susan Gordon lives in New York City, and is originally from Rome, Italy. She holds an MFA in creative writing from the New School.

PHOTO CREDITS

Cover, pp. 1, 36 © Hulton/Archive/Getty Images, Inc.; pp. 4, 15, 23, 24, 34 © Bettmann/Corbis; pp. 6, 8, 11, 12, 14, 16, 20, 37, 38 © The Everett Collection; p. 21 © Underwood and Underwood/Corbis; pp. 25, 31 © The Hulton-Deutsch Collection/Corbis; p. 27 © AP/Wide World Photos; p. 28 © Archivo Iconografico/Corbis.

Designer: Thomas Forget; Editor: Charles Hofer